Be Not Afraid

Words of Hope and Promise

The Reverend Alanson B. Houghton

Phoenix Press

WALKER AND COMPANY

New York

This book is dedicated
to my father and others I love
who have gone on ahead of me
into the land of our Lord

All Scripture quotations are from the King James Version

Copyright © 1988 by Alanson B. Houghton

All rights reserved. No part of this book may be reproduced or transmitted in any form or by any means, electronic or mechanical, including photocopying, recording, or any information storage-and-retrieval system, without permission in writing from the Publisher.

Printed in the United States of America.

Library of Congress Cataloging-in-Publication Data

Houghton, Alanson B.
   Be not afraid.

   1. Death—Religious aspects—Christianity.
2. Consolation. I. Title.
BT825.H78 1988   242'.4   88-5917
ISBN 0-8027-2612-7

Send for a complete catalog of large-print publications.

CONTENTS

INTRODUCTION

Much has been written to help those who mourn deal with grief and loss. Little has been written to help those of us—in fact *all* of us—who face death in the near or distant future. Hence this "road map" for you and me as we face the inevitable certainty and one of the great mysteries of our existence—*Death*.

In over twenty years as a parish priest, I have talked to fewer than a dozen parishioners about their own impending deaths, yet I have counseled hundreds who have been left behind. This seems all backwards. You would think that we would want to explore the possibilities, "talk around" the subject of our own death, or at least share our fears with someone we trust and respect. But it just doesn't seem to work out that way. We clam up. We refuse to talk about it. In some cases, I'm sure, we won't even think about it. Maybe, possibly, hopefully, we might want to read about it!

I am scared "of" death but I am not scared "to" death, and there is a huge difference. I don't want to leave the familiar, the seen, the known, the people I love and the people who love me. No one looks forward to taking a one-way trip, all alone, regardless of how adventuresome it's cracked up to be. It is a scary thought, and we put it off as long as we possibly can.

On the other hand, we have been told by Jesus: *"Be not afraid."* (Matt. 28:10). He said this first to a group of disciples who stood open-mouthed and disbelieving outside his tomb. He says it again to us who are just as bewildered and wondering as they were. The Risen Jesus is the most profound evidence that there is life beyond our physical death, that God's promise to us of a life without ending rather than a life that simply ends with death is a reality, not a panacea or a hoax. Others have written on this, and some have alluded to dying and then coming back filled with wonder and hope about what lies ahead. But to me the most compelling evidence of all is presented in the Four Gospels; different stories from different authors at different times with different viewpoints but *all* certain about one fact—Jesus died but lived again. And so will we!

The whole point of Christianity is that God entered the world he had created, and shared our condition as a flesh-and-blood human being who went through all the stages of human life from birth to death. No pretending. No escaping the worst that can happen to human beings —suffering and death. Yet out of the reality and gloom that surrounded Jesus' death came the gradual realization that what he had said, he meant!

He that believeth in me, though he were dead, yet shall he live.

John 11:25b

Jesus had a real sense of hope, otherwise he wouldn't have said such things. Note his own words from the Cross:

Father, into thy hands I commend my spirit.

Luke 23:46b

These words underline his own conviction that God would somehow fold him into his arms and take him home. He died on a Cross of pain but turned it into a Cross of promise. In some new and wondrous way *he lived*, and because of that so would we when it came time to close our eyes in death. That was and still is the Good News of the Gospels.

Helen Keller is reported to have said:

> I cannot understand why anyone should fear death. Death, which at heart is life eternal, reunites and reconciles. I believe that when the eyes within my physical eyes shall open on the world to come, I shall simply be consciously living in the country of my heart.

I don't want to leave my present post, but I am both curious and challenged that life, in its broadest sense, does go on. If I believe what I preach and literally stake my life on it, death will be overcome and I will live on with God and those I love in what C.S. Lewis and others have called my true country.

But even Professor Lewis was realistic

about our apprehensions. Note this marvelous passage from *Christian Behaviour*:

Most of us find it very difficult to want "Heaven" at all—except insofar as "Heaven" means meeting again our friends who have died. One reason for this difficulty is that we have not been trained: our whole education tends to fix our mind on this world. Another reason is that when the real want for Heaven is present in us, we do not recognize it. Most people, if they had really learned to look into their own hearts, would know that they do want, and want acutely, something that cannot be had in this world. There are all sorts of things in this world that *offer* to give it to you, but they never quite keep their promise. The longings which arise in us when we first fall in love, or first think of some foreign country, or first take up some subject that excites us, are longings which no marriage, no travel, no learning, can really satisfy.[1]

This little book contains my own musings, passages from both the Old and New Testaments, and what others have written. It was put together to help me muddle through the dark nights of the soul that we all experience as we grow older, have heart attacks, discover cancer, contract AIDS, or just become depressed and worn out. If we can believe what the Psalmist sings—

I shall not die, but live . . .

Psalm 118:17

—if we can believe that death does not close the door on what we have experienced or what we hope for, then we can plan ahead! We can think and wonder and muse and pray about this new adventure, this new life which lies just around the corner.

A friend of mine who died from complications of multiple sclerosis in his mid-forties said to his wife a week before he died, "I want to go home." He wasn't in the hospital. He was in his own bed. He was packed and ready. I'd like to be packed and ready when it comes my time to "go home"—into that place where I shall spend the rest of my life, my eternity.

Death

is a Reality-

Not a Failure

1

When my father died I received the following note from Will Campbell —preacher, writer, and friend:

Dear Alan: My Mamma died and we buried her at East Fork on New Year's Day. I heard your Papa died, too. Somebody's always leaving. In the Community. Will.

Somebody *is* always leaving. Yesterday it was a parent or a spouse or a friend. Tomorrow it could be you or it could be me. Our death is a certainty. The only uncertainty is how and when. We need to pull that out of the recesses of our minds and into the forefront of our consciousness—not to dwell on but to deal with—in ways which admit to its reality, defuse its terror, and help us look at our own death through the eyes of faith.

Benjamin Franklin wrote this letter to his niece in 1752:

I condole with you. We have lost a dear and valuable relation. But it is the will of God and nature, that these mortal bodies be laid aside, when the soul is to enter into real life. This is a rather embryo estate, a preparation for living.

A man is not completely born until he is dead. Why then should we grieve that a new child is born among the immortals, a new member is added to their happy society? We are spirits. That bodies should be lent us, while they can afford us pleasure, assist us in acquiring knowledge, or in doing good to our fellow creatures, is a kind and benevolent act of God. When they become unfit for these purposes, and afford us pain instead of pleasure, instead of an aid become an encumbrance, and answer none of the intentions for which they were given, it is equally kind and benevolent that a way is provided by which we may get rid of them. Death is that way.

Our friend and we were invited abroad on a party of pleasure, which is to last for ever. His chair was ready first, and he is gone before us. We could not all conveniently start together; and why should you and I be grieved at this, since we are soon to follow, and know where to find him.[2]

Franklin's words take the abject sense of failure out of death. He doesn't avoid death's reality, but he puts it in terms of birth, change, release, even an invitation!

What will our own death be like? Probably not like in the movies or in most books. I believe we'll just go to sleep and wake up somewhere else! The French call sleep *petit mort* (little death) for we do lose consciousness when we are asleep. In fact, we experience a little death every single night! Maybe that is God and Nature's way of preparing us, of easing our fear; of helping us look at our death simply as a "passing" from one place to another.

I remember climbing into a Pullman berth years ago, looking out the window until I fell asleep, and then waking to a new day, in a new place. There was a definite separation from yesterday and the station where I had boarded the train, but there was also an excitement and cer-

tainty about where I now was disem-
barking. I just hope my own death, my
ride through the night, will be something
like that!

I am standing upon the seashore. A
ship at my side spreads her white sails
to the morning breeze and starts for the
blue ocean. She is an object of beauty
and strength, and I stand and watch her
until, at length, she hangs like a speck of
white cloud just where the sea and sky
come down to mingle with each other.
Then someone at my side says, "There!
She's gone."

Gone where? Gone from my sight—that
is all. She is just as large in mast and hull
and spar as she was when she left my
side, and just as able to bear her load of
living freight to the place of destination.
Her diminished size is in me, not in her;
and just at the moment when someone
at my side says, "There! She's
gone"—there are other eyes watching
her coming, and other voices ready to
take up the glad shout, "Here she comes!"

(author unknown)

So death is a journey into a new

place—a new consciousness—a new state of being where all the paraphernalia we have collected and used for life as we know it is not appropriate. When we move to a warmer climate we don't take an overcoat. When we move into our new life we don't take our old body. That covering was for another climate, another place, another time.

We like our bodies, whatever their shape or condition, because that's all we know. We are loath to give them up! But death requires that we travel light. When we arrive in our true country I am sure we'll be "reclothed" in proper attire for that place and clime. Bodies are like envelopes. They contain the letter, the spirit, the essence of what we really are. We don't save envelopes but we rarely forget what was said in the letters they carried. So in death our envelopes, our bodies, are discarded, for they are no longer necessary to carry our spirit, the eternal us. *That goes on and lives on!*

Tagore, Indian poet and philosopher, wrote:

Death is not extinguishing the light—it

is putting out the lamp because dawn has come.

A new day. A new light. A new chance. A new body. A new life. Death, seen in that perspective, seems far less threatening, far less of a failure. Its reality hasn't gone away, nor are we foolish enough to think we can take a later train. But it no longer seems unnatural *or* unfair. Death is a door we simply must go through when our work is done.

O Lord, support us all the day long of this troublous life, until the shadows lengthen, and the evening comes, and the busy world is hushed, and the fever of life is over, and our work is done. Then, in thy great mercy, grant us a safe lodging, and a holy rest, and peace at last.[3]

Fear and Hope -

Opposite Sides

of the

Same Coin

2

Goodman Ace told this story to Norman Cousins, who then published it in the *Saturday Review*:

A man, having a premonition about his death, asked his minister whether there was any way of gaining assurance he would go to heaven, which he felt was laid out like a golf course and where he would get to play every day. In fact, he said, he was prepared to leave his entire fortune to the church if he knew in advance that he was destined for the upper zone.

Several days later the minister telephoned. "I have good news and bad news. First, the good news. I can assure you without qualification that you are going to heaven."

"Wonderful," said the man. "Now, what is the bad news?"

"You tee off next Thursday at 10:15 A.M."

We laugh at tales like this because it is how we cope with our fear of dying! We need to keep our sense of humor as we cope with what lies ahead—particularly the unpleasant fact that one of these days (maybe not next Thursday) *we are going to die*. I underline and repeat this, for I am convinced we are more frightened by what we imagine than what we know for a fact.

I had a friend who was diagnosed as having lung cancer. He said he felt better once he knew specifically what was wrong, and he faced his operation with incredible calm and courage. He admitted being scared about the pain and the long-term prognosis, but as he said, "Either I am in charge or the cancer is!" He wasn't talking about *length* of life but *quality* of life. He was assuming control of his own well being rather than letting the terror of cancer cripple him above as well as below the neck.

Bishop Charles Henry Brent, who stayed with my grandparents in London during his final illness, wrote:

What peace to live in the knowledge that we need not worry about the terrors of death as we look ahead and anticipate our last hour; if we but trust now we shall be able to trust with a practical faith then, as Christ trusted, and there will be "light at evening time." Christ, who in Himself conquered death, will repeat His victory in us and for us. . . .

I have the quiet consolation, steadily growing, that death is only an incident, and that its power has been so broken that it can do little else than create a momentary break in inter-communication. Love somehow becomes more of a steady flame through death.

That is the ultimate statement of one who lived in certain hope of the Resurrection, in certain hope that his death was to be anticipated, not avoided, and that God in Jesus had showed death for what it was—a momentary break, a change of direction, the storm before the calm, the road to a life without end. Julius Lester echoes Bishop Brent—in his own words, taken from *Do Lord Remember Me*:[4]

Death is nothing but a walk into the light.

13

I read an article in the *Episcopalian* taken from a taped interview by Wilbur L. Scranton III with his wife Jane two months before she died. He has given me permission to include it here. What she says in this excerpt has helped me deal with my own fears and also be more open to the hope *and* promise that Christ holds out to us all.

I feel if I had died suddenly, I would have been cheated. So many of us say we'd rather go quickly, that there's probably not much pain, not much preparation, not much worry, that it's hard for the grieving relatives but probably terrific for the person who dies.

I don't feel that way now. I feel that if that happened to me, I would have lost out on one of the most important growing experiences in my life. The past few years have been tremendous. In my relationship with my husband, I think I might have felt cheated if we had not worked everything out, if we had not grown together as we should have, if we had not grown in our love of the Lord. But having this time to face these things together, we have become more honest with one another, more willing to get inside each other, and we have a much richer marriage because of it.

With the pain and all I've been through—I know it sounds crazy, but I just have to say it—I've been blessed. The Lord is seeing me through it all. He's helped me through each of the difficult situations.

I used to think of the dates, the holidays, the seasons. I used to say, "Well, the buds are coming; I wonder if I'll be around next year when the buds come out," or "All the leaves are turning color now; I wonder if I'll be around when the leaves come out on the trees." I'm not thinking those kinds of thoughts at all any more. I'm really taking one day at a time, I really know that the Lord is going to take care of whatever the details have to be at the end. I'm not going to be concerned whether it's going to be convenient for everybody. It's probably not going to be convenient for anybody. A couple of weeks ago when I heard the doctors say that things were starting to go faster, that it didn't seem as if any of the medications were doing anything, it was with a great sense of relief that I said, "It's going to be sooner. I'll be with the Lord."

Sometimes I get excited. It's like planning a terrific trip, and I've got all the tickets and everything's ready to go. The only drawback is I don't know when I'm leaving. Maybe because I'm getting closer to when the trip's going to take place, I'm getting more excited—because I know the time is coming faster, and I'm not going to have to wait a lot longer to cash in that ticket.

Maybe that's the reason I'm more at peace. That's the anticipation of the Christian—being with the Lord. That really does get you excited if you truly believe in the Resurrection. I hope and pray that everyone left behind has a transition as smooth and peaceful as mine is going to be.

Someone commented that when Dr. Salk discovered a cure for polio millions of people waited in line to be vaccinated in order to be sure they would live. Why then don't we take Jesus seriously when he tells us:

Whosoever liveth and believeth in me shall never die.

John 11:26a

Jane Scranton did!

16

Martin Luther wrote:

I know not what the future holds but I know who holds the future.

That simple declaration of faith in a God who cares and delivers on his promises is more than a play on words. It is the basis on which we are able to say, as we close our eyes each day in sleep or in death:

Lord, into thy hands I commend my spirit.

adapted from Luke 23:46

17

The Will
to Live -
The Willingness
to Die

3

Lord, help us enjoy the blessings of this day . . . and the fears bear patiently and sweetly; for this day is ours; we are dead to yesterday and we are not yet born to the morrow.

(author unknown)

We live one day at a time. We learn from the yesterdays and dream about the tomorrows. Today is all-encompassing and requires all our energy and attention. Whether sick or well, calm or troubled, scared or excited, our will to live is what motivates and moves us from minute to minute, place to place.

I have been on two airplanes that had to make emergency landings. In one case I put my head between my knees in preparation for a crash landing, and in the other I looked out the window at the fire trucks and ambulances lined up alongside the fast-approaching runway. In both cases we landed safely, but my will to live, before I knew that, was incredibly strong. I admit that those familiar words from the Twenty-third Psalm tempered my fear somewhat—enough to be a very scared but wondering participant rather than screaming helplessly. I felt exactly the same way when I was rolled into the operating room for the removal of what was thought to be a malignant tumor.

The Lord is my shepherd; I shall not want.

He maketh me to lie down in green pastures: he leadeth me beside the still waters.

He restoreth my soul: he leadeth me in the paths of rightousness for his name's sake.

Yea, though I walk through the valley of the shadow of death, I will fear no evil: for thou art with me; thy rod and thy staff they comfort me.

Thou preparest a table before me in the presence of mine enemies: thou anointest my head with oil; my cup runneth over.

Surely goodness and mercy shall follow me all the days of my life: and I will dwell in the house of the Lord for ever.

Though I walk through the valley of the shadow of death, I will fear no evil: For thou art with me; thy rod and thy staff they comfort me.

We all walk through the valley of the shadow of death every single day. The two key words are "walk" and "shadow." Our will to live keeps us walking, moving through whatever is our part and parcel today. We also know that the shadow of dying is our constant companion, whether we are terminally ill or about to jaywalk across a crowded street in New York! We really don't know exactly when or how we may die; but the hopeful, positive, faithful sides of our nature propel us beyond our fears and enable us to live out each particular moment without a pervading sense of gloom.

We may feel terrific. We may feel awful. But in both extremes our will to live gives us enormous energy. And what makes this possible—at least for me—is the deep conviction that God is with me.

The Lord will protect me. God is around! I am not alone. Whatever happens I'll be OK, and in his inscrutable way he will hold me close.

The will to live and the grace and courage with which we live are measures of our dual belief—in our own dignity and in God's divinity—and in that shared responsibility for our present and our future. Ted Ferris, one-time Rector of Trinity Church, Boston, left us this prayer to help us through our day, whatever it may be.[5]

This is another day. I know not what it will bring forth, but make me ready, Lord, for whatever it may be.

If I am to stand up, help me to stand bravely.

If I am to sit still, help me to sit quietly.

If I am to lie low, help me to do it patiently.

And if I am to do nothing, let me do it gallantly.

Make these words more than words, and give me the Spirit of Jesus.[5]

In the St. Paul's School Chapel Service

Book is a prayer which leads me into thinking about how and when we should give ourselves or those we love permission to die!

God of our weary years, God of our silent tears; Thou who has brought us thus far on our way; Thou who hast by thy might lead us into the light, Keep us forever in the path, we pray.

If we really believe that death is nothing but a walk into the light, then the closure of one chapter and the beginning of another are natural events. There also comes a time when letting go is not only timely but merciful. The hard part is being able to let go and let God take over, to paraphrase an old Alcoholics Anonymous expression.

I am talking about the willingness to die and then giving ourselves *or* those we love permission to do just that! We all hang onto life for a lot of complicated reasons, but part of that tenacity has to do with our concern for those we'll leave behind when we begin our new life. Somehow we have to come to the realization that they will be fine, and somehow they have to assure us that this is really true.

I hope my own deeds will match my words when it is my time to let go. Dying can be a scary business, but if our faith in God, in ourselves, *and* in those we must leave behind is intact, then it may be easier to lay down this life in order to pick up our new one. Pain is always a motivator, but Peace—a sense that we are not alone, a sense that we are loved, a sense that whatever happens everyone will be just fine—is what makes the real difference.

I can remember reading part of Psalm 139 to my father a couple of nights before he died, at his request! It was his way, I think, of getting ready to let go and let God take over. I have watched a lot of people die and I am convinced that at some point they knew and welcomed the release and looked forward to the adventure—for they fell asleep in death as if their hand was already firmly clasped by someone on the other side. Here is the Psalm as I read it to my father:

O LORD, thou hast searched me, and known me.

Thou knowest my downsitting and mine uprising, thou understandeth my thought afar off.

Thou compassest my path and my lying down and art acquainted with all my ways.

For there is not a word in my tongue, but, lo, O LORD, thou knowest it altogether.

Thou hast beset me behind and before, and laid thine hand upon me.

Such knowledge is too wonderful for me; it is high, I cannot attain unto it.

Whither shall I go from thy spirit? or whither shall I flee from thy presence?

If I ascend up into heaven, thou art there: if I make my bed in hell, behold, thou art there.

If I take the wings of the morning, and dwell in the uttermost parts of the sea;

Even there shall thy hand lead me, and thy right hand shall hold me.

If I say, Surely the darkness shall cover me; even the night shall be light about me.

Yea, the darkness hideth not from thee;

but the night shineth as the day: the darkness and light are both alike to thee.

For thou hast possessed my reins: thou hast covered me in my mother's womb.

I will praise thee; for I am fearfully and wonderfully made: marvelous are thy works; and that my soul knoweth right well.

My substance was not hid from thee, when I was made in secret, and curiously wrought in the lowest parts of the earth.

Thine eyes did see my substance, yet being unperfect; and in thy book all my members were written, which in continuance were fashioned, when as yet there was none of them.

How precious also are thy thoughts unto me, O God! how great is the sum of them.

If I should count them, they are more in number than the sand: when I awake, I am still with thee.

Search me, O God, and know my heart: try me, and know my thoughts:
And see if there be any wicked in me, and lead me in the way everlasting.

Psalm 139:1–18, 23–24

We may have to give permission to die to someone we love very much. We must convince them that we'll be OK, that we'll miss them a lot, *but* that we'll make it! That is how we "tell them" that it is all right to let themselves go into the hands and land of their Lord.

We are trying to communicate what the author of Psalm 73 felt:

> Whom have I in heaven but thee? And having thee, I desire nothing else on earth. Though heart and body fail, yet God is my possession forever.

That speaks of faith in a living, loving God.

In another way we are trying to say to them what someone said to me:

> Like the forsythia blooming in your backyard, man, too, has his seasons. Your father has passed beyond his winter. But in you, sons and daughters, he leaves a remarkable spring.

That made (and makes) a huge difference to me—knowing that I too will eventually leave something of myself behind—almost like carving my initials into a tree. We must let those we love know they are firm in our memories and that we are grateful for that special part of themselves that they are leaving deep within us. We must let them know we are sad for us but glad for them as they begin their new and exciting life with God.

Death
is the End
of One Chapter
and the Beginning
of Another

4

In the book *I Heard the Owl Call My Name*,[6] there is a scene toward the end where an old Indian woman is looking out a window, thinking about the young priest who just died. He served them well. He knew he was dying. He was faithful to the end. She whispers to no one in particular:

Walk straight on, my son, and don't look back. You are going into the Land of your Lord.

I find myself whispering these same words when I hear of the death of a friend. They acknowledge the fact of death but reaffirm the promise of a larger, longer life. We go through a door into another room. Endings are also beginnings!

I had a friend die here in Charleston who knew she was going to die, didn't like it one bit, but did want to talk about it. One day she blurted, "Alan, I thought I was going to live forever." I blurted right back, "Lib—you got it! You're right. You *are* going to live forever." *And we are!* That is what keeps me going and keeps me sane. If I didn't believe that death was only a horizon and that beyond it is a new life, a new me, and a new you in Christ, I would be totally devoid of hope.

Bishop Warren Chandler was asked just before he died: "Do you dread to cross the river of death?" He replied, "My Father owns the land on both sides of the river. Why should I fear?" It is faith like that which topples any and all specious arguments. It is faith like that which carries and leads us through our own valleys of doubt and dread.

We overcomplicate and overthink the simple and direct promises of the Gospels. Jesus came and went and came again, and so shall we. Never mind the details. God holds out his hand and offers to walk us through the door that leads from this life into the other. Everything we touch or taste or see has an ending, but later we touch and taste and see something new. We come. We leave. We come back. We are born. We die. We live. It's really that simple and that profound!

> We seem to give him back to thee, dear God, who gavest him to us. Yet, as thou didst lose him in giving, so we have not lost him by his return. Not as the world giveth, givest thou, O Lover of souls! What thou givest thou takest away. For what is thine is ours always, if we are thine.
>
> And life is eternal; and love is immortal; and death is only a horizon; and a horizon is nothing save the limit of our sight.
>
> Lift us up, O God, that we may see further; cleanse our eyes that we may see more clearly; draw us closer to thyself, that we may know ourselves nearer to our beloved who are with thee.[7]

I like this life a lot. I also look forward to the next. If I can keep both in some sort of healthy balance, I'll be better able to close one door with grace and open the other with courage.

I realize that trusting in ourselves or in God isn't that easy. It's largely a matter of faith in the promises of God *and* in the logical, natural processes of life. Look at the caterpillar and what happens. One life comes to a close, and a new one—in fact a more beautiful one as a butterfly —begins. We marvel at that. Why can't we marvel at the fact that we are promised the same metamorphosis, the same transformation, as we go "from life to life"?

Ted Ferris gives us another prayer that may ease our worries about our journey at life's end (or better said—at life's beginning!).

O God, we know that all things work together for good to them that love thee; we know that though we walk through the valley of the shadow of death, thou art always with us, and that there is nothing to fear but the loss of thee; we know that nothing can separate us from those we love, and that in thy safe keeping they are free from danger and harm. Knowing these things, O God, may we go quietly forward from day to day, not looking too far ahead, taking each step with the confidence that what we are asked to do or bear, for that thou wilt give us the strength we need. Amen.

God does give us the strength, through his promise and his presence, if we will permit him to enter our fearful and wondering hearts. We are loath to give up control. We have become so sophisticated that we question everything. We insist on proof. The one assurance you'd think we'd embrace without question —God's promise of life without ending, with him, in Paradise—we question and we doubt. We may explore it in church, but when pressed we still have lingering doubts. *Why?* It is literally the promise of a lifetime, yet we turn away and hedge our bets.

I try to focus on the empty Cross. Either it means nothing or it means everything. Either it's a grim reminder of a miscalculation, an unnecessary and cruel death, or it means that God has done exactly what he promised, that Jesus lives, and because of that so will you and so will I. We have to "die" to get there, but we have to "die" to do a lot of other things in the course of our present lives, such as growing up and growing old.

The other way I deal with death is to look at the other options: darkness, nothing, The End, *Finis!* I simply cannot believe that life is senseless, and that all I have learned here isn't preparation for a longer existence somewhere beyond my sight and knowledge. Even if my lot is a tough one and the evidences of hope in everyday life are dim, I hold onto the hope that this wondrous creation with its countless manifestations has its being, its breadth, its depth, its beginnings somewhere outside my limited range.

Life may seem senseless at times, but when we consider its dimensions, it *is* utterly amazing! Look at the love of one person for another, the way trees change color and recreate their foliage. Look at silent tadpoles becoming noisy frogs, pigeons taken miles from their homes easily finding their way home. Look at how what we discard fertilizes the earth from which springs new life. A creation like this is *recreative;* therefore there *must* be more. Death may be our way of making way, of fertilizing, of changing our color and our form so that nature may continue its miracle. If this is so, and I deeply believe it is, then I have nothing to fear when darkness comes.

My hair is gray—it once was brown. My years number well over fifty—once they numbered less than five. My teenage years ended, my young adult years began. You see how the cycles of life we take for granted are really no different than what's ahead. It's just that our eyesight isn't 20/20 when it comes to what lies around the corner.

We can see endings with a lot more clarity than we can spot beginnings. It's not what's out there that is unclear, it is our sight. I accept limitation. I also accept that my present life must come to a close before my new life can begin! Those are the facts. All I need to do is match them with my faith that God will keep his promises—and I deeply believe that he will.

Death's but a path that must be trod,
If a man would ever pass to God.

Thomas Parnell (1679–1718)

Where
the
Old Testament
Points Us

5

The Old Testament is a book of many parts: history, prophecy, poetry, laws, inspiration. It reminds us over and over again that we are God's people and that he does care a lot. The Bible is the Word of God written in the words of human beings. This makes it easier to relate to, for those same men and women who put it together also faced the same uncertainties in life and the same certainty of their own deaths that you and I do. In fact their existence was more marginal than ours, so the specter of death was more of a daily companion.

In the Book of Samuel there is an extraordinary story that describes the conviction that we eventually do follow those we love into some sort of future life. It also sets an example for dealing with the reality of death itself:

And Nathan departed unto his house. And the Lord struck the child that Uriah's wife bare unto David, and it was very sick. David therefore besought God for the child; and David fasted, and went in, and lay all night upon the earth. And the elders of his house arose, and went to him, to raise him up from the earth: but he would not, neither did he eat bread with them. And it came to pass on the seventh day, that the child died. And the servants of David feared to tell him that the child was dead: for they said, Behold, while the child was yet alive, we spake unto him, and he would not hearken unto our voice: How will he then vex himself, if we tell him that the child is dead? But David saw that his servants whispered, David perceived that the child was dead: therefore David said unto his servants, Is the child dead? And they said, He is dead. Then David arose from the earth, and washed, and anointed himself, and changed his apparel, and came into the house of the Lord, and worshipped: then he came to his own house; and when he required, they set bread before him, and he did eat.

Then said his servants unto him, What thing is this that thou hast done? Thou didst fast and weep for the child, while it was alive; but when the child was dead, thou didst rise and eat bread. And he said, While the child was yet alive, I fasted and wept: for I said, Who can tell whether God will be gracious to me, that the child may live? But now he is dead, wherefore should I fast? Can I bring him back again? I shall go to him, but he shall not return to me.

2 Samuel 12:15–23

Job, who suffered every possible loss and indignity, never lost his trust in God's ultimate fairness *and* that God lived and because of that so would he in one way or another. The nineteenth Chapter of Job is a triumphant statement of that conviction:

I know that my redeemer liveth, and that he shall stand at the latter day upon the earth: And though this body shall be destroyed, yet I shall see God: Whom I shall see for myself, and mine eye shall behold, and not as a stranger!

Job 19:25–27

The Psalms, the ancient Hebrew hymnal, is one of the most human books in the entire Bible. The writers of the Psalms capture our moods, our concerns, our hopes, our fears, our ups and our downs, as we struggle with our humanity while at the same time acknowledging God's incredible love for each and every one of us. The Psalms are full of promises that God will not desert us or simply leave us to our fate.

As for me, I will behold thy face in righteousness: I shall be satisfied, when I awake, with thy likeness.

Psalm 17:15

I will lift up mine eyes unto the hills, from whence cometh my help.

My help cometh from the Lord, which made heaven and earth.

He will not suffer thy foot to be moved: he that keepeth thee will not slumber.

Behold, he that keepeth Israel shall neither slumber nor sleep.

The Lord is thy keeper: the Lord is thy shade upon thy right hand.

The sun shall not smite thee by day, nor the moon by night.

The Lord shall preserve thee from all evil: he shall preserve thy soul.

The Lord shall preserve thy going out and thy coming in from this time forth, and even for evermore.

Psalm 121

In Ecclesiastes, there is a wonderful poem about life's seasons that balances all the movements and moments of human existence. If we believe that "every activity" is "under heaven" then God's plan for us *must* have a longer, more eternal view.

To every thing there is a season, and a
     time for every purpose under
     heaven:
A time to be born, and a time to die;
A time to plant, and a time to pluck up
     that which is planted;
A time to kill, and a time to heal;
A time to break down, and a time to
     build up;
A time to weep, and a time to laugh;
A time to mourn, and a time to dance;
A time to cast away stones, and a time
     to gather stones together;

A time to embrace, and a time to refrain
from embracing;
A time to get, and a time to lose;
A time to keep, and a time to cast
away;
A time to rend, and a time to sew;
A time to keep silence, and a time to
speak;
A time to love, and a time to hate;
A time of war, and a time of peace.

Ecclesiastes 3:1–8

The prophet Isaiah is more specific about our eventual deliverance into an eternal life:

And he will destroy in this mountain the face of the covering cast over all people, and the veil that is spread over all nations.

He will swallow up death in victory; and the LORD GOD will wipe away tears from off all faces; and the rebuke of his people shall he take away from off all the earth: for the LORD hath spoken it.

And it shall be said in that day, Lo, this is our God; we have waited for him, and he will save us: this is the LORD; we have waited for him, we will be glad and rejoice in his salvation.

Isaiah 25:7–9

Thy dead men shall live, together with my dead body shall they arise. Awake and sing, ye that dwell in dust: for thy dew is as the dew of herbs, and the earth shall cast out the dead.

Isaiah 26:19

Ezekiel is more graphic and promises a definite resurrection:

Therefore prophesy and say unto them, Thus saith the LORD GOD; Behold, O my people, I will open your graves, and cause you to come up out of your graves, and bring you into the land of Israel.

And ye shall know that I am the Lord, when I have opened your graves, O my people, and brought you up out of your graves.

And shall put my spirit in you, and ye shall live, and I shall place you in your own land: then shall ye know that I the Lord have spoken it, and performed it, saith the Lord.

Ezekiel 37:12–14

Although not in the Old Testament, these nine verses from the Apocryphal

Book of Wisdom renew my faith in God's plan for me—and that a new life with him, because of his grace and mercy, will actually be mine! *Thanks be to God!*

But the souls of the righteous are in the hand of God, and there shall no torment touch them.

In the sight of the unwise they seemed to die: and their departure is taken for misery,

And their going from us to be utter destruction: but they are in peace.

For though they be punished in the sight of men, yet is their hope full of immortality.

And having been a little chastised, they shall be greatly rewarded: for God proved them, and found them worthy for himself.

As gold in the furnace hath he tried them, and received them as a burnt offering.

And in the time of their visitation they shall shine, and run to and fro like sparks among the stubble.

They shall judge the nations, and have dominion over the people, and their Lord shall reign forever.

They that put their trust in him shall understand the truth: and such as be faithful in love shall abide with him: for grace and mercy is to his saints, and he hath care for his elect.

Wisdom 3:1–9

What the New Testament Promises Us

6

The New Testament—the new prom-ise—needs less of an introduction to Christians. Its entire message—the Good News of God in Christ—is a testament that God *is* larger than life; that life as we know it is but a few score years within a much larger time frame; that Jesus' birth, life, death, and Resurrection were the most dramatic and personal way God could convince us that life really was ev-erlasting! Jesus' own words to Martha and Mary after their brother Lazarus had died sum it up in two sentences:

Jesus said unto her, I am the resurrec-tion, and the life; he that believeth in me, though he were dead, yet he shall live; And whosoever liveth and believeth in me shall never die.

John 11:25–26

Jesus follows this immediately with a question to Martha: Believest thou this? She answers: Yes, Lord. *What is our answer?*

Other reminders that life does go on come from John's Gospel. Jesus said:

> Verily, verily, I say unto you, he that heareth my word and believeth on him that sent me, hath everlasting life, and shall not come into condemnation; but is passed from death unto life.
>
> John 5:24

> And this is the Father's will which hath sent me, that of all which he hath given me I should lose nothing, but should raise it up again at the last day. And this is the will of him that sent me, that every one which seeth the Son, and believeth on him, may have everlasting life: and I will raise him up at the last day.
>
> John 6:39–40

> Let not your heart be troubled: ye believe in God, believe also in me. In my father's house are many mansions: if it were not so, I would have told you. I go to prepare a place for you. And if I go and prepare a place for you, I will come again,

and receive you unto myself; that where I am, there ye may be also. And whither I go ye know, and the way ye know. Thomas saith unto him, Lord, we know not whither thou goest; and how can we know the way? Jesus saith unto him, I am the way, the truth, and the life: no man cometh unto the Father, but by me.

John 14:1–6

One of the nagging questions that troubles believers and nonbelievers alike is that narrow statement "No man cometh unto the father, but by me." In the first-century religious context that Jesus was reflecting, that statement was prophetic, *not* pedantic.

Jesus makes *my* understanding of God and my individual faith a lot more focused and real, and it is through *his* life and death and Resurrection that it all becomes clear for me. But I have Jewish and Buddhist friends for whom this is of little meaning, yet their hope for immortality, for a life without ending, is as strong as mine! I am convinced we all end up in the land of our Lord. I'm also convinced that the knowledge of and belief in Jesus makes that final awakening a more acceptable experience. But the words of that William Cowper hymn written in 1774 alert me to the fact that "God moves in a mysterious way His wonders to perform" and that "Blind unbelief is sure to err, and scan His work in vain; God is His own interpreter, and He will make it plain."

It was hard for the disciples to "see" Jesus after he rose from the dead, to believe that the unbelievable had actually happened, to have living proof that life really did go on even if on a different plane. It is also very hard for us to accept him and what he lived for and died to prove. It is difficult for us to make that necessary leap of faith. Look at the problem Mary Magdalene had!

But Mary stood without at the sepulchre weeping; and as she wept, she stooped down, and looked into the sepulchre. And seeth two angels in white sitting, the one at the head, and the other at the feet, where the body of Jesus had lain. And they say unto her, Woman, why weepest thou? She saith unto them, Because they have taken away my Lord, and I know not where they have laid him. And when she had thus said, she turned herself back, and saw Jesus standing, and knew not that it was Jesus. Jesus saith unto her, Woman, why weepest thou? She, supposing him to be the gardener, saith unto him, Sire, if thou have borne him hence, tell me where thou hast laid him, and I will take him away. Jesus said unto her, Mary. She turned herself, and saith unto him, Rabboni; which is to say, Master.

John 20:11–16

The disciples experienced the same struggle. They had a terrible time coping with Jesus' death, much less any serious consideration of a resurrection. But there he was, and they had to cope with that reality. Slowly they began to more fully sense his presence, and their own words and actions began to ring out with the truth of a deeper, growing faith.

Paul the Apostle expresses it by far the best:

What shall we say then? Shall we continue in sin, that grace may abound? God forbid. How shall we, that are dead to sin, live any longer therein? Know ye not, that so many of us were baptized into Jesus

Christ were baptized into his death? Therefore we are buried with him by baptism into death: that like as Christ was raised up from the dead by the glory of the Father, even so we also should walk in newness of life. For if we have been planted together in the likeness of his death, we shall be also in the likeness of his resurrection: Knowing this, that our old man is crucified with him, that the body of sin might be destroyed, that henceforth we should not serve sin. For he that is dead is freed from sin. Now if we be dead with Christ, we believe that we shall also live with him: Knowing that Christ being raised from the dead dieth no more; death hath no more dominion over him. For in that he died, he died unto sin once: but in that he liveth, he liveth unto God. Likewise reckon ye also yourselves to be dead indeed unto sin, but alive unto God through Jesus Christ our Lord.

But if the spirit of him that raised up Jesus from the dead dwell in you, he that raised up Christ from the dead shall also quicken your mortal bodies by his Spirit that dwelleth in you.

Romans 6:1–11; Romans 8:11

But now is Christ risen from the dead, and become the firstfruits of them that slept. For since by man came death, by man came also the resurrection of the dead. For as in Adam all die, even so in Christ shall all be made alive. But every man in his own order: Christ the firstfruits; afterward they that are Christ's at his coming.

But some man will say, How are the dead raised up? and with what body do they come? Thou fool, that which thou sowest is not quickened, except it die: And that which thou sowest, thou sowest not that body that shall be, but bare grain, it may chance of wheat, or of some other grain: but God giveth it a body as it hath pleased him, and to every seed its own body. All flesh is not the same flesh: but there is one kind of flesh of men, another flesh of beasts, another of fishes, and another of birds. There are also celestial bodies, and bodies terrestrial: but the glory of the celestial is one, and the glory of the terrestrial is another. There is one glory of the sun, and another glory of the moon, and another glory of the stars: for one star differeth from another star in glory. So also is the resurrection of the dead. It is sown in corruption; it is raised in incorruption: It is sown in dishonour; it is raised in glory: it is sown in weakness; it is raised in power: It is sown a natural body; it is raised a spiritual body. There is a natural body, and there is a spiritual body.

Now this I say, brethren, that flesh and blood cannot inherit the kingdom of God; neither doth corruption inherit corruption. Behold, I show you a mystery; We shall not all sleep, but we shall all be changed, In a moment, in the twinkling of an eye, at the last trump: for the trumpet shall sound, and the dead shall be raised incorruptible, and we shall be changed. For this corruptible shall have put on incorruption, and this mortal must put on immortality. So when this corruptible shall have put on incorruption, and this mortal shall have put on immortality, then shall be brought to pass the saying that is written, Death is swallowed up in victory. O death, where is thy sting? O grave, where is thy victory? The sting of death is sin; and the strength of sin is the law. But thanks be to God, which giveth us the victory through our Lord Jesus Christ.

1 Cor. 15:20–23; 35–44; 50–57

We having the same spirit of faith, according as it is written, I believed, and therefore have I spoken; we also believe, and therefore speak; Knowing that he which raised up the Lord Jesus shall raise up us also by Jesus, and shall present us with you.

2 Cor. 4:13–14

The second Letter of Peter makes it clear that our life here on earth—its depth and breath—is preparation for what is to come in the eternal kingdom. There is a definite demand for a commitment, a buying in, a serious stab at taking God as seriously as we take ourselves. *All the New Testament writers agree that faith is the key to the kingdom.*

Like the huddled figures sitting in the dark cave in Plato's *Republic,* we must accustom ourselves to the love and light of Christ so we will not only know where we are going but where we are when we get there! This life is a training ground for the next, just like the teenage years are a training ground for adulthood. We learn, we change, we graduate from one stage into another and the quality of each is some measure of the seriousness of our desire to live on with God for an eternity.

According as his divine power hath given unto us all things that pertain unto life and godliness, through the knowledge of him that hath called us to glory and virtue: Whereby are given unto us exceeding great and precious promises: that by these ye might be partakers of the divine nature, having escaped the corruption that is in the world through lust. And beside this, giving all diligence, add to your faith virtue; and to virtue knowledge; And to knowledge temperance; and to temperance patience; and to patience godliness; And to godliness brotherly kindness; and to brotherly kindness charity. For if these things be in you, and abound, they make you that ye shall neither be barren nor unfruitful in the knowledge of our Lord Jesus Christ. But he that lacketh these things is blind, and cannot see afar off, and hath forgotten that he was purged from his old sins. Wherefore the rather, brethren, give diligence to make your calling and election sure: for if ye do these things, ye shall never fall: For so an entrance shall be ministered unto you abundantly into the everlasting kingdom of our Lord and Saviour Jesus Christ.

2 Peter 1:3–11

At the very end of the Bible, in fact the second to the last sentence in the Book of Revelation 22:20, are there six words: *Amen. Even so, Come Lord Jesus.* It is the cry of the curious and the hopeful. It is the plea of those who want to be with Christ and in Christ, today, tomorrow, and forever. It is the prayer of hope that we can live out each day in certain hope of the Resurrection—his and ours!

For God so loved the world, that he gave his only begotten Son, that whosoever believeth in him should not perish, but have everlasting life.

John 3:6

Therein lies His promise, our hope, and the Peace that really does pass all understanding:

O God, who hast made us the creatures of time, so that every tomorrow is an unknown country, and every decision a venture of faith,

Grant us, frail children of the day, who are blind to the future, to move toward it with a sure confidence in your love, from which neither life nor death can separate us.

Reinhold Niebuhr—
Forward Day by Day

All is Well!

7

An English parson wrote these words of hope many years ago:

Death is nothing at all . . . I have only slipped away into the next room. . . . I am I and you are you . . . whatever we were to each other that we are still. Call me by my old familiar name, speak to me in the easy way you always used. Put no difference into your tone; wear no forced air of solemnity or sorrow. Laugh as we always laughed at the little jokes we enjoyed together. Play, smile, think of me, pray for me. Let my name be ever the household words that it always was. Let it be spoken without effect, without the ghost of a shadow on it. Life means all that it ever meant. It is the same as it ever was; there is absolutely unbroken continuity. What is this death but a negligible accident? Why should I be out of mind because I am out of sight? I am but waiting for you, for an interval, somewhere very near just around the corner. . . . All is well.

Canon Henry Scott
Holland (1847–1918)

All is well! That's the point, that's the hope, and that's the lens through which we must view our death. *We are not taken "from" but taken "to"!* "Just around the corner" is a wonderful metaphor, for our distance from each other will not be that great.

God has not taken them from us. He has hidden them in His heart that they may be closer to ours.

I like those words penned to me by a close friend. Time, space, distance, all the constraints of human life simply don't apply to God's country!

I have a cousin, Adelaide Griswold, who is writing a book. In it is a chapter which deals with the death of her first husband and her difficulty in letting him go even though she is now happily remarried. It fits into what I am trying to say, and I have her permission to share it:

To my astonishment, I discovered, I was not only grieving over Frank's death, I was grieving over mine. The person Frank thought me to be was, in a very real sense, as dead as he. No one would ever see me through his eyes ever. The children and my friends knew me well and I loved them for their insight, but Frank was my touchstone. It was to his vision of me that I responded for twenty-four years. He alone could keep it alive. I now believe he took his vision of me with him when he died. It's really a nice thought. He's keeping his me alive up there and I'm keeping my him alive down here. It's also a very useful theory for second marriages. I can be with Frank and Brendan forever, alone, and at the same time. Each man will have his own me so there will be no ghastly running back and forth and choosing. Nor will I have to see Brendan's face when he sees his first wife Kathryn again. Her Brendan is already up there.

All *is* well! The more we think about

it, the closer we come to our own death, the clearer we need to be about the journey. Here are two prayers that mean a lot to me. John Donne (1571–1631) wrote the first. I have no idea who wrote the second.

Bring us, O Lord God, at our last awakening into the house and gate of heaven, to enter into that gate and dwell in that house, where there shall be no darkness nor dazzling, but one equal light; no noise nor silence, but one equal music; no fears nor hopes, but one equal possession; no ends nor beginnings, but one equal eternity; in the habitations of thy glory and dominion world without end.

Weak are we all and dying, O God; give us thy peace, strength for life's battle while it lasts, and rest at the close of day when work is done. Keep us beneath the shadow of thy great protection, till, o'er the hills of time, the angels of thy glory sing again.

John Heywood (1497–1580) in *Proverbes* wrote, "All is well that endes well. All *is* well that ends well, and that is what happens to you and me when we face up to the end of our present life. I knew a man who got up one Tuesday morning and put on his Sunday best. He asked his son to take him to the hospital because he wasn't feeling well. They went. He died within the hour. He got all dressed up as if he was about to take an important trip. *He was and he did!*

When Jesus raised Lazarus from the dead, his first words to Martha and Mary were "Let him go" (John 11:44). I think he meant just that—let him go on into his new life, let him loose, don't hang on, let him go and let him be with God.

I used this brief prayer at a funeral service: "Lord, as our friend begins her new life with you, help us to begin our new lives without her!" *We* had to let her go. All was now well for her *and*, in another sense, for us! All is well—and will be well—if we can firmly put ourselves in God's hands—for the todays *and* the tomorrows!

Nothing Can
Separate Us
From the
Love of God

8

For as many as are led by the Spirit of God, they are the sons of God. For ye have not received the spirit of bondage again to fear; but ye have received the Spirit of adoption, whereby we cry, Abba, Father. The Spirit himself beareth witness with our spirit, that we are the children of God; And if children, then heirs; heirs of God, and joint-heirs with Christ; if so be that we suffer with him, that we may be also glorified together. For I reckon that the sufferings of this present time are not worthy to be compared with the glory which shall be revealed in us. For the earnest expectation of the creature waiteth for the manifestation of the sons of God.

Who is he that condemneth? It is Christ that died, yea rather, that is risen again, who is even at the right hand of God, who also maketh intercession for us.

Who shall separate us from the love of Christ? shall tribulation, or distress, or persecution, or famine, or nakedness, or peril, or sword? Nay, in all these things we are more than conquerors, through him that loved us. For I am persuaded, that neither death, nor life, nor angels, nor principalities, nor powers, nor things present, nor things to come, nor height, nor depth, nor any other creature, shall be able to separate us from the love of God, which is in Christ Jesus our Lord.

Romans 8:14–19; 34–35; 37–39

I agree with Saint Paul. *Nothing* can separate us from the love of God which is in Christ Jesus our Lord. We are not only more than conquerors, we are victors in the battle for life. The prize we all seek, another and continuing life with him, is within our grasp. Death is but a change in the natural order. Death is the means by which we travel from one life to the next, a rite of passage to a greater maturity, a deeper peace, a more fulfilling existence unhampered by the vicissitudes of our present humanity. What keeps us calm and expectant is the sure knowledge that our Lord is with us *every single step* of the way.

Most of us are born into this world out of a union of love between parents we did not choose but who did choose us. In a sense we came from the unknown into the known. Someday we will be called upon to take another journey, a trip into another place where the same legacy of love, magnified a thousand times, awaits us. Again it's not our choice but the choice of a God who loves us enough to allow us to be reborn into a far, far better world.

We have no memory of our time in our mother's womb or even of our very early years; but we were cared for, loved, and allowed to grow. We have little knowledge of what next awaits us, except through the prayers and writings and faith of those who have preceded us. The most compelling evidence of all is the fact that Jesus travelled the same road first himself. He was scared, as we are. He asked that it be put off, as we do. He even had moments on the Cross where he felt he had been abandoned, as we will. But God came through as he had promised, and through the vale of death emerged a risen Lord who evidences for us the fact of eternal life—what is literally right around the corner.

There is a story about a German sailor writing home to his mother during the first World War:

> If you hear that my ship has been sunk do not fear. The seas into which my body sinks are the hands of my Saviour from which nothing can separate me.

What a promise! What a comfort to know that whatever happens to us we are in God's hands. When we die to this world, he delivers us from the womb of our present existence and brings us as a newborn child of God into a new life that never ends.

John Donne said in one of his famous sermons at St. Paul's in London:

> When I die I shall see God. And when I have seen Him, I shall never die.

Death does not close the door on life; in

fact, it opens another life, and opens our eyes to a reality beyond our wildest dreams.

You and I must each face our own death alone. We can't expect too much from those who love us so much they can't bear the thought of our moving on. We must forgive them and pray for them because *they* are the ones left behind when we begin our new lives.

As Benjamin Franklin reminded us, we are invited abroad on a party of pleasure which is to last forever. We travel hand in hand with Him who loves us. We are expectant. We are ready. We will go to sleep in death and awaken to a new day, an eternity with Him who loves us more than we can possibly comprehend.

Do not be afraid. Death does not close the door on life.

Remember me, O Lord, according to the favor which thou bearest unto thy people; and grant that increasing in knowledge and love of Thee, I may go from strength to strength in the life of perfect service in thy heavenly kingdom; through Jesus Christ Thy Son, my Lord.

from *The Book of Common Prayer*

EPITAPH

Someone once told me that a long obituary was the sign of a short life! I'm not sure I agree, but I am sure we all want to be remembered in one way or another.

We'll be too busy in our new life to be scanning the papers for what people say, or too involved to eavesdrop on our own service. Therefore, I decided to frame my own epitaph, not for posterity but to remind me *now* what I ought to be doing in this life in preparation for the next.

I come from a family whose gravestones are flat to the ground, unencumbered other than the names and the dates of arrival and departure. Therefore these words will not appear anywhere except in this book. Here is what I hope my present life reflects:

HE LOVED
   HE CARED
      HE SERVED
        HE BELIEVED

I close this book with a hymn I have known since childhood. It made me a little bit sad then and it still does. But it also calms me, assures me, comforts me, and gives me the courage and confidence to travel on into the tomorrows, whether they be here with you *or* there with him.

Now the day is over,
Night is drawing nigh,
Shadows of the evening
Steal across the sky.

Jesus, give the weary
Calm and sweet repose;
With thy tenderest blessing
May our eyelids close.

Grant to little children
Visions bright of thee;
Guard the sailors tossing
On the deep, blue sea.

Comfort every sufferer
Watching late in pain;
Those who plan some evil
From their sin restrain.

Through the long night watches
May thine angels spread

Their white wings above me,
Watching round my bed.

When the morning wakens,
Then may I arise
Pure, and fresh, and sinless
In thy holy eyes. Amen.

Sabine Baring-Gould, 1865
(Hymnal-1940)

NOTES

1. From *Christian Behavior* by C. S. Lewis (New York: Macmillan, 1950).

2. Benjamin Franklin's letter is excerpted in *A Book of Condolences* by Rachel Harding and Mary Dyson (New York: Continum, 1981).

3. Quotation is from the contribution of John Henry Newman, (1801–1890) to *The Book of Common Prayer*.

4. Excerpt from Julius Lester, *Do Lord Remember Me* (New York: Holt, Rinehart, and Winston, 1984).

5. From Ted Ferris, *Book of Prayers for Everyman* (Greenwich Conn.: Seabury, 1962).

6. *I Heard the Owl Call My Name* is by Margaret Craven (Dell, 1988).

7. From *Burial Services* (Wilton, CT: Bernandin, Morehouse, and Barlow, 1980).